DISCOVER THE *KEY PRINCIPLE* TO UNLOCK

KINGDOM SUCCESS IN YOUR LIFE.

THE
GRAIN
PILE
PRINCIPLE

GARY KEESEE

TABLE OF CONTENTS

INTRODUCTION

HOW DID THIS HAPPEN?

The Lord was with Joseph so that he prospered.

—Genesis 39:2a

Right now, even if you are in the midst of an impossible situation, you can prosper. Even if you are surrounded by ungodly people who know nothing about God. Even if your circumstances are so bad today that you can't imagine how things could get worse. None of that matters. You can prosper.

How do we know this?

Because it happened for Joseph.

In the first book of the Bible, Genesis, we see Joseph growing up in a large dysfunctional family. His brothers hated him and wanted to kill him. In fact, they tried to kill him.

But the Lord was with Joseph. At the last minute, his brothers changed their minds and sold Joseph to a passing caravan of Ishmaelites. The traders took him down to Egypt and sold him as a slave to Potiphar, who was one of Pharaoh's top officials and the captain of his guard.

But Joseph was a descendant of Abraham, who had a covenant with God. So, the Lord was with Joseph and prospered him.

Joseph did such a fantastic job for Potiphar that he was soon running the entire estate.

Later on, Potiphar's wife tried to seduce Joseph—and when he resisted, she falsely accused him of attempting to rape her. Joseph landed in a prison cell.

Again, the Lord was with Joseph and prospered him in prison. The prison warden soon put Joseph in charge of all the other prisoners.

One day, something unusual happened. The guards came for Joseph. They got him bathed, shaved, and then brought him before Pharaoh.

Again, the Lord was with Joseph in his meeting with Pharaoh. Within minutes, Pharaoh had put Joseph in charge over Egypt—at that time the mightiest kingdom on the face of the earth. The Lord prospered Joseph, and he saved not only the nation of Egypt but also the lives of his family.

So, here was a man who found himself in one impossible situation after another—and yet each time the Lord prospered him and exalted him into a place of honor and leadership.

I always like to say we need to be "spiritual scientists." So, as spiritual scientists, our first question ought to be: "How did this happen?"

Seven Preliminary Observations

Before we examine Joseph's story for clues as to why and how he prospered in the midst of these impossible situations while surrounded by ungodly people, let's make a few preliminary observations.

First, since the Bible tells us that the Lord was with Joseph and he prospered, it's reasonable to conclude that if the Lord is with us, then we will also prosper.

Second, if the Lord is with us and we are *not* prospering, then we might conclude that something is wrong with our "default settings," and our lives have not "booted up" properly.

Third, this means that instead of allowing our circumstances to dictate our potential, we just need to change our "default settings" to correspond with what God says is true about our lives.

Fourth, we see that Joseph was born of royalty, born for royalty, and born with the blessing of God. Since he was a descendant of Abraham, he was included in the covenant made by his great-grandfather, which allowed heaven to be legally involved in his life.

Fifth, if we are also descendants of Abraham, then we are also included in the same covenant. Therefore, the blessing of God is also our legal right as citizens of the Kingdom of God.

Sixth, if the Lord is with us because we are part of the covenant, then we can forget about whatever impossible situations we may find ourselves in today. We don't have to worry about the ungodly people around us. Where we came from does not matter.

Finally, since this means you have a legal right to the blessing of heaven, if you will follow the example of Joseph and act on the same principles we see demonstrated in his life, then you can anticipate that the Lord will prosper you and, like Joseph, you will be exalted and promoted to a great, great place!

CHAPTER
ONE

STEPPING INTO GOD'S PLAN

Joseph's story—like all of our stories—begins with Adam and Eve in the Garden.

In the beginning, Adam and Eve were created on the earth to rule the earth realm; and as you know, they committed treason and fell. So, they lost their position. They lost their provision. Satan deceived them, and as a result, they lost their authority in God's Kingdom.

So, God had to find another man to bring His government into the earth realm, someone else who would be able to influence the earth realm on behalf of His government.

The Lord chose Abram, who later became Abraham. Abraham obeyed God and made a covenant with Him. A covenant is a legal agreement that binds both parties to the promises they make to one another. This covenant with Abraham opened the door to restore the legal jurisdiction of heaven in the earth realm.

This covenant was with Abraham and all of his descendants. Throughout the rest of the Bible, we watch as this legal agreement is passed along from generation to generation.

This also explains why the New Testament begins with a genealogical record. Many people skip over this list of names when they are reading the Bible because it seems boring to them. But the fact is that genealogical record in the first chapter of the Gospel of Matthew is crucial because it tracks the lineage of Jesus. This is proof to Satan that Jesus is legally the heir of Abraham within the earth realm, and thus Jesus had every right to enter the earth realm.

From Good to Bad to Worse

Joseph was born into this covenant of blessing. He was the great-grandson of Abraham, the grandson of Isaac, and the son of Jacob (who later became Israel); and he was the second youngest of 12 brothers.

But things had gotten off to a bad start for Joseph. He was rejected and abandoned by his brothers. He found himself in Egypt where he was not part of the right ethnic group. Genesis 43:32 says it was detestable to an Egyptian to even eat a meal with a Hebrew.

And Joseph had been sold into slavery. As a slave in the house of Potiphar, Joseph found himself in an impossible situation, surrounded by ungodly people, and apparently with no hope for the future.

But Joseph's story doesn't end there.

> *The Lord was with Joseph so that he prospered, and he lived in the house of his Egyptian master. When his master saw that the Lord was with him and that the Lord gave him success in everything he did, Joseph found favor in his eyes and became his attendant. Potiphar put him in charge of his household, and he entrusted to his care everything he owned.*
>
> —Genesis 39:2-4

I find it interesting that Potiphar noticed that the Lord was with Joseph. Potiphar wasn't Jewish. He didn't know God. And as you know, God is invisible. So, how is it that Potiphar "saw" that God was with Joseph?

What happened was that Potiphar observed the quantity and quality of Joseph's work—and he recognized that the Lord was giving Joseph success in every task he handled. So, Potiphar promoted Joseph on the basis of what he saw him do and who he was.

Before long, Potiphar promoted Joseph to oversee his entire household—and because Joseph carried the blessing of God, Potiphar's household was blessed as well.

From the time he put him in charge of his household and of all that he owned, the Lord blessed the household of the Egyptian because of Joseph. The blessing of the Lord was on everything Potiphar had, both in the house and in the field. So Potiphar left everything he had in Joseph's care; with Joseph in charge, he did not concern himself with anything except the food he ate.

—Genesis 39:5-6a

What's Holding You Back?

You need to pay close attention to this story, particularly if you do not feel you are prospering in the way that Joseph prospered—because, as we've seen, if God is with you, you should expect to prosper.

Joseph was a slave, but the Lord was with him. He was working in the house of the ungodly, working in a position with no future and no potential, but the Lord prospered him.

So, it's time for you to leave your "victim mentality" behind. You may have come from a bad background, but so did Joseph. It's time to leave that behind you. Maybe you've been mistreated by others or cheated by someone. It's time to put that in the past.

You may not fit in for some other reason. Joseph didn't fit in. His own brothers wanted to kill him and sold him into slavery. So, you need to forget how you were rejected and abandoned. You need to forget how disloyalty has hurt you in the past or how you've suffered at the hands of those you trusted. You need to forget the injustice and brush off the false accusations.

You need to forget about the hopeless situation you're in. Joseph was in prison with no way out, but God had a plan for his life. And God has a plan for your life too. But you have to be willing to step into that plan and stop dwelling on who you think you are.

If you ran into Adam and Eve at some point after the Fall, you would have thought they were losers. They had some pretty serious family issues. One of their sons murdered the other. They lost their home, they lost their provision, and they were living in poverty, just surviving by their painful toil and sweat.

But this wasn't what God had intended for them. This wasn't their created purpose. Before the Fall, Adam and Eve ruled the world. They were of royal descent.

So, you have to stop looking at yourself from the perspective of where you are right now. You need to think about your created purpose. Instead of looking at yourself from the perspective of who you think you are, you need to look at yourself the way God designed you to be.

God made you for a special purpose. He made you to rule in life. Like Joseph, there is royal blood in your veins.

You may recall that when Joseph was young, he told his brothers about some dreams he had been having that one day he would rule over them. Although this annoyed his brothers, I believe those dreams encouraged Joseph during his hard times. He knew that the Lord was faithful and that He would not leave him there forever.

At the time, Joseph didn't know *what* would happen, *when* it would happen, or *how* it would happen—but he knew that God knew where he was. And so Joseph remained faithful to God because he knew he would one day come out of those situations.

What dreams are you holding on to these days? We can think of a dream like a picture. If I asked you to close your eyes right now and think about yourself, what picture do you see?

A lot of people see themselves in negative ways. "Well, I'm not good-looking," they might say. "I'm overweight." "I don't have money." And what they think of when they look in the mirror is that they don't like to look at themselves in the mirror.

Friend, you have to get over that.

You are a child of God. You have been made in God's image, and you are special. And until you recognize that, no one else will.

Our dreams are important. When my daughter Polly was very young, we asked her what she wanted for Christmas. She said, "I want a cash register."

I thought it was kind of strange. "Why do you want that, Polly?"

"Because someday, I'm gonna own my own hair salon, and I want to run a cash register."

Now, if you've met my daughter, you know she now has her own hair salon and she has a cash register.

She also used to say that one day, she would marry a boy she knew, Jon Patton. She never told Jon that, but that was her dream her entire life. And if you've met her husband, you know that she married Jon Patton.

Those are true stories. Pretty amazing, aren't they?

So, what are your dreams? When you were a kid, did you ever sit around with your brothers or sisters or cousins and talk about what you wanted to be when you grew up?

When you were young, you had dreams. I know I did. My daughter did. Yet, many of us somehow let life beat those dreams out of us.

But those dreams are still alive. God is the one who made you a dreamer.

You may be aware of the actress Sarah Jessica Parker. She grew up in Nelsonville, Ohio, which is not far from where Drenda and I live now. I've heard her talk about how she grew up on welfare. Her family was very poor. They didn't have electricity. Sometimes, their phone was cut off. They didn't have money for birthday parties. She spent her childhood watching her parents shuffle and try to pay the bills.

Now, her net worth is estimated to be $200 million.[1]

The author J.K. Rowling was a single mom living on welfare in the UK. She has said she was as poor as possible without being homeless. She often wrote in a café, writing by hand because she didn't have enough money to buy a typewriter.[2] Early in her career, a literary agent told her that it was not possible to make very much money writing children's books.[3]

Now, she's worth over a billion, making her one of the richest authors in the world.

Are you letting your past hold you back? You need to just put all that aside. Like Joseph, we all have stories. We all come from someplace. You need to lay that all behind and set your sights forward—because you have a great future ahead of you!

1. Allen Lee, "How Sarah Jessica Parker Achieved a Net Worth of $200 Million," https://www.moneyinc.com, January 29, 2023.
2. https://www.folkloreforkids.blogspot.com/2022/02/jk-rowlings-life.html
3. Jani, "J.K. Rowling's advice for (content) writers," https://www.blog.flipsnack.com, May 9, 2017.

CHAPTER
TWO

WHEN NOBODY KNOWS YOUR NAME

Now, let's get back to Joseph. Was his journey a fluke? A lucky break? A coincidence?

I don't think so. It's obvious that God was leading him, that God was with him, and that's why he prospered. But I think Joseph's actions also played a big role.

First, when we say that the Lord was with Joseph, what does that mean? Someone may ask, "Isn't God with everyone?"

Well, that's almost a trick question. The answer is no. Because God is *not* with everyone. He loves everyone. He desires to be with everyone. But that does *not* mean He is with them now.

> *Therefore, remember that formerly you who are Gentiles by birth and called "uncircumcised" by those who call themselves "the circumcision" (which is done in the body by human hands)—remember that at that time you were separate from Christ, excluded from citizenship in Israel and foreigners to the covenants of the promise, without hope and without God in the world. But now in Christ Jesus you who once were far away have been brought near by the blood of Christ.*
>
> —Ephesians 2:11-13

*Consequently, you are no longer foreigners and strangers,
but fellow citizens with God's people and also members of
his household.*

—Ephesians 2:19

So, when the Scriptures say that God was with Joseph, this is primarily a reference to Abraham's covenant, which is what made it legal for God to be with Joseph and to bless him in the earth realm.

It's important for us to understand that the Lord was with Joseph *only* because Joseph had a covenant with God. This was made possible *only* by the legal agreement with God established through the lineage of his great-granddad, Abraham.

Remember, Adam and Eve found themselves essentially bankrupt because they had committed treason against God.

But Abraham was very wealthy—acquiring *"sheep and cattle, male and female donkeys, male and female servants, and camels"* (Genesis 12:16)—because he was in this covenant with God.

It is being in covenant with God that brings the blessing of the Lord.

Later, as Moses led the children of Israel out of Egypt and into the Land of Promise, he paused to remind them of this fact.

> *You may say to yourself, "My power and the strength of my hands have produced this wealth for me." But remember the Lord your God, for it is he who gives you the ability to produce wealth, and so confirms his covenant, which he swore to your ancestors, as it is today.*
>
> —Deuteronomy 8:17-18

Sometimes when we hear this Scripture preached today, the emphasis is on how God gives us the ability to produce wealth so that we can preach His covenant (the Gospel). But notice that's not what the verse says. What it says is that our ability to prosper actually *confirms* the covenant that we have with God.

Of course, we always want to financially support the proclamation of the Gospel. But what this Scripture is saying is that the blessing of the Lord—the blessing that Abraham had, the blessing that Joseph had—will have an impact on your finances because God has made a legal agreement to prosper you.

You Will Be Blessed

We should also take note that once Potiphar put his entire household under Joseph's authority, something pretty amazing happened.

> *From the time he put him in charge of his household and of all that he owned, the Lord blessed the household of the Egyptian because of Joseph. The blessing of the Lord was on everything Potiphar had, both in the house and in the field.*
>
> —Genesis 39:5

It is crucial to understand that the blessing of the Lord is based on the promises of God. We see this clearly in Deuteronomy 28, the chapter of blessing:

> *If you fully obey the Lord your God and carefully follow all his commands I give you today, the Lord your God will set you high above all the nations on earth. All these blessings will come on you and accompany you if you obey the Lord your God:*
>
> > *You will be blessed in the city and blessed in the country.*

The fruit of your womb will be blessed, and the crops of your land and the young of your livestock—the calves of your herds and the lambs of your flocks.

Your basket and your kneading trough will be blessed.

You will be blessed when you come in and blessed when you go out.

The Lord will grant that the enemies who rise up against you will be defeated before you. They will come at you from one direction but flee from you in seven.

The Lord will send a blessing on your barns and on everything you put your hand to. The Lord your God will bless you in the land he is giving you.

—Deuteronomy 28:1-8

In this passage, Moses is talking about the prosperity that comes from the covenant of blessing—the promises, the oath—that God established with Abraham. If the people remain faithful to the covenant, in the same way that Potiphar saw that the Lord was with Joseph, the whole world will see that God is abundantly prospering His people.

The Lord will establish you as his holy people, as he promised you on oath, if you keep the commands of the Lord your God and walk in obedience to him. Then all the peoples on earth will see that you are called by the name of the Lord, and they will fear you. The Lord will grant you abundant prosperity—in the fruit of your womb, the young of your livestock and the crops of your ground—in the land he swore to your ancestors to give you.

—Deuteronomy 28:9-11

This is the inheritance of all of Abraham's descendants, which means it is also your legal destiny. It is who you are. This is how your life should look.

So, you cannot continue to look at yourself based on Adam and Eve's fall and see yourself as your weaknesses and your problems and where you came from. That's not who you are!

You have to go back to see how Adam and Eve were created to live because that's how you were created to live. You have been given the promises of God. He's the God who made everything—and it is impossible for Him to lie. Let that sink in.

The blessing of Abraham is found not only in the Old Testament but also in the pages of the New Testament. Jesus has made a way for the blessing of the Lord to be reestablished in your life. You are also included in Abraham's covenant when you receive the promises of God by faith.

> *Christ redeemed us from the curse of the law by becoming a curse for us, for it is written: "Cursed is everyone who is hung on a pole." He redeemed us in order that the blessing given to Abraham might come to the Gentiles through Christ Jesus, so that by faith we might receive the promise of the Spirit.*
>
> —Galatians 3:13-14

The promises God made with Abraham have no end. His descendants throughout the whole earth would be blessed. And now through Jesus Christ, the blessing of Abraham extends beyond our lives here in the earth realm. In fact, we have a better covenant—"*since the new covenant is established on better promises*" (Hebrews 8:6).

And now, since you have been restored back to God, you have the Spirit of God living in you. You are a child of God. You have the *blessing* of Abraham, but you also have the *life* of Jesus Christ. You are alive to God!

The Lord was with Joseph, and He prospered him. He is also with you—but He is more than just *with* you; the very spirit of God dwells *within* you.

You are the temple of the Holy Spirit. The Bible says you have the mind of Christ (1 Corinthians 2:16), the wisdom of God (Colossians 1:9), and you can do all things through Christ who strengthens you (Philippians 4:13).

Jesus said, *"Everything is possible for one who believes"* (Mark 9:23).

Since all of this now belongs to us, instead of asking, "What we can do to prosper?" our question should be, "With all of this, how can we *not* prosper?"

Of course, we have some learning to do. We have to grow in these things. And we will all make mistakes. But the Bible says, *"Though the righteous fall seven times, they rise again"* (Proverbs 24:16a). We won't stay down because we have promises of God—and our focus is on those promises and not on where we've been.

So, What's the Problem?

"Well, Pastor," someone might say, "I just don't see much of this happening in my life."

That's the problem. You're waiting to see it. But you don't just wait for blessing. That never works. What does God bless? He blesses what you put your hands to.

> *The Lord will open the heavens, the storehouse of his bounty, to send rain on your land in season and to bless all the work of your hands.*
>
> —Deuteronomy 28:12

So, here's a question for you: If God is doing His part—if He is opening the heavens, sending rain, and blessing the work of your hands—would you rather raise three tomato plants or 50,000 tomato plants?

> *You will lend to many nations but will borrow from none. The Lord will make you the head, not the tail. If you pay attention to the commands of the Lord your God that I give you this day and carefully follow them, you will always be at the top, never at the bottom.*
>
> —Deuteronomy 28:12b-13

If you have the blessing, you're not going to be thinking in terms of survival. If whatever you put your hand to will be blessed, you won't be saying, "Let me raise three really great tomato plants."

What you will be thinking instead is: *I'm the head, not the tail. I'm the lender, not the borrower. I need more land, so I can raise tomatoes by the truckload!*

You need to stop thinking too small—thinking like a slave— and start thinking like who you are. You are God's child. You have the blessing. And you have endless potential—for God *"is able to do immeasurably more than all we ask or imagine, according to his power that is at work within us"* (Ephesians 3:20).

Not only did the Lord bless everything Joseph put his hand to but also we see that Potiphar was blessed as well. *"The blessing of the Lord was on everything Potiphar had, both in the house and in the field"* (Genesis 39:5b).

And right now, there's a whole world full of Potiphars out there looking for God. But they're not going to see God until someone demonstrates to them what God's Kingdom looks like.

So, if there's a short circuit somewhere, it's not on God's part. It's in your thinking. You have to think differently, talk differently, and walk differently.

Although God can do more than you can ask or imagine, it's also true that you'll never ask for more than you can imagine. And you'll never imagine something you think is impossible. Which is why you're content with raising three tomato plants and not dreaming about raising 50,000.

Several years ago, I was invited to speak at a church, and two teenagers came up to me and told me about a fantastic idea they had for an app they wanted to develop. (Doesn't everyone?) But a year later I was back at that church, and those same kids came running up with big smiles on their faces.

"Well, it's almost finished," they told me. "We have a million dollars in the bank from the investors that are funding the development of the app, and we have some buyers lined up and ready to buy it when it's finished."

Imagine! These kids were only 17 years old—with a million dollars in the bank and buyers standing by. These were just two teenagers who heard about the Kingdom of God.

Is there any reason why you can't do something like this? Like what? Too many family problems? Too many failures in your past?

At one of our recent Provision Conferences, one of our partners told her story.

She and her husband owned several companies that were struggling financially. They had run through their resources and savings.

Their main business was new construction, and they specialized in high-end properties. She told me they had clients that wanted them to build apartment communities, but they couldn't get loans. So, everybody was sitting around, and nobody was making any money.

Then one day, she was watching Sid Roth's show when I was his guest on the program. She sent me an email. "Pastor Gary, we're struggling, but we don't believe in going bankrupt. We don't want to do that. Do you have any sage words of wisdom?"

So, I emailed her with a few of my thoughts, and we invited her to one of our conferences. They lived in Dallas, but she and her husband flew to Columbus and spent three days with us.

I'll let her describe what happened next.

> The third day, Gary spoke over everyone in the audience and said, "Go to lunch, and we're going to believe God's going to give you a million-dollar idea."
>
> My husband and I went to lunch and sat down. I said, "I have this idea." My husband is an artist, so he sketched out the idea at lunch. It was a new product line that we later launched through our advertising firm. Last year alone, it did close to a million dollars. And since then, of course, it's made well over a million dollars.
>
> It's changed our lives to know that God can download a million-dollar idea to you.

So, what changed for that couple? We gave her permission. Of course, I'm certain she could have done the same thing in the month before she came to our conference. Because she already had the promises. God was standing by. He was ready to give her million-dollar ideas.

But it wasn't until the conference that she realized who she was—and that's when her whole life changed. That's when the lightbulb went off.

What You Practice in Private

One more thing we should note about Joseph is he was put in charge of Potiphar's household when he was a slave. He started on the bottom rung. Nobody cared about him. Nobody knew his name.

How you handle your life when no one knows your name determines if someone will ever know your name.

Joseph had a dream. He was faithful to God. He had set God as his source. He had no way to promote himself—no web page, no Facebook. So, he was going to trust God. He was going to be faithful. He was going to operate with integrity and handle every detail with excellence.

Even when he was falsely accused and went to prison, he operated in integrity—and he ended up running the prison.

So, what do we see happening here? Joseph practiced handling responsibility. He practiced operating with integrity. So, when the time came that he stood before Pharaoh, he had already been running various things for a long time.

It's the same with the destiny God has for you. He is going to give you the chance to practice before people know your name. That way, you can make mistakes and no one will know about them. They will just be between you and God. He's going to help you. You just have to operate in integrity.

Joseph purposed in his heart that he was going to operate with integrity at all times. He worked faithfully while he was a slave to Potiphar. He could have been bitter at his brothers or bitter at God, but instead he gave everything he did his best effort.

It was the same during his time in prison. He could have let himself be bitter about being falsely accused, but instead he set himself with God as his source and operated with integrity.

And it's the same for you. When you go to work, you want your employers to say that you are the very best employee they've ever had. Your whole goal as an employee is to make your employer money.

Someone may say, "No, Pastor—my whole goal is to make me money!"

But that's missing the point. If you work with integrity and the goal of making them money, you will make money—because

God will make sure it also happens for you.

I was flying home from a conference in Houston late one Friday night. My pilot, Stephen, let me know that we didn't have enough fuel to get us all the way to Columbus, so we'd be making a stop in Louisville.

So, we landed and fueled up the usual FOB, and the lady rang it up. The guy brought her the sheet, she looked at it, and then she looked at the computer. "Hmm," she said, "something's not right here."

But eventually, she gave the total, we paid, went out to the plane, and took off without a problem. But then we got up to about 15,000 feet, and the left fuel tank went dry. Two or three minutes later, the right tank went dry.

We were at 15,000 feet. No gas. Not good.

So, it turned out the lady was right—something was wrong. For whatever reason, they didn't put any fuel in the plane.

It was night. It was dark. Stephen started looking for a runway. As you can imagine, you only get one shot at something like this.

Fortunately, Stephen's a great pilot, and he was able to glide the plane down for a perfect landing.

The point I want to make with this story is that this wasn't the first time Stephen has done this. You mean it happens often? No, it doesn't. Stephen told me this had never happened to him in his whole career.

But it's not the first time he has done it. He has practiced landing a plane without engines hundreds of times over the past 20 or so years. And what you practice in private has a big impact on what happens in public.

More Than You Can Ask or Imagine

People often ask me why I talk about money as much as I do.

The reason I teach about money is so that you can be free from the fear of not having it and free from the greed of it. Because when you're at peace and you have money to pay your bills, you can think about other, more important things—like serving God, like helping people, like having a great marriage.

When Drenda and I were living under stress over money, we found it suffocated life. One of the reasons I talk about money a lot is because I went through nine years of suffocation, antidepressants, and panic attacks. And I wouldn't wish that on my favorite enemy.

But in Christ, you have every promise. The Bible says, *"For no matter how many promises God has made, they are 'Yes' in Christ"* (2 Corinthians 1:20a).

You have the blessing of Abraham. You have the blessing of being a son or daughter of God. The Holy Spirit in you has all the answers you need. The promises of God apply to every area of life—your health, your marriage, your finances, every area. And in all things, God will bless whatever you put your hand to immeasurably more than you can ask or imagine. It's like God is giving you a blank check!

CHAPTER
THREE

THE BLESSING OF THE LORD

Let's review Joseph's situation at this point in his story. He was a slave in the home of an Egyptian official, an ungodly man, in a nation that hated God and worshipped a pantheon of other gods. And yet Joseph prospered.

I hear Christians complain all the time that they don't like where they work. "It's so dark and sinful," they say. "Everyone cusses and carries on, and there's so much garbage going on there."

But guess what? You *can* prosper there. Joseph was a slave and had no rights, yet he prospered to the degree that Potiphar saw the uniqueness about his life—and that's why Potiphar chose him to rule his entire estate.

Like Joseph, you are to look different. You are to prosper in the midst of impossible situations and among the ungodly who know nothing about God.

How did Potiphar see God? Had Joseph been reading Scriptures to him? No, Potiphar saw *success*. And why did Joseph have success? The Bible says it was the blessing of the Lord.

The blessing of the Lord in our lives is the byproduct of the covenant that God made with Abraham. Remember, a covenant is a legal agreement that contains promises—and these promises are part of the blessing of Abraham.

So, Joseph had the legal right to this blessing and these promises because He was in the lineage of his great-grandfather. God was involved in his life, and he prospered in the midst of his dire personal circumstances.

What Is the Blessing of the Lord?

It's worth remembering that we have these same promises available to us because the blessing of Abraham has come upon the Gentiles through Jesus Christ.

> *Christ redeemed us from the curse of the law ... He redeemed us in order that the blessing given to Abraham might come to the Gentiles through Christ Jesus.*
> —Galatians 3:13a-14a

The Jewish faith came to the Gentiles through Jesus Christ, and so did the covenant, which means that you now have the blessing of Abraham.

The blessing of Abraham involves the earth realm. It overrides the earth curse that came when Adam sinned and resulted in men and women having to make their way through life by their own painful toil and sweat.

But now, you should prosper—because the blessing of Abraham has restored God's involvement in your life within the earth realm.

But you also have obtained another level of blessing:

> *Consequently, you are no longer foreigners and strangers, but fellow citizens with God's people and also members of his household.*
>
> *—Ephesians 2:19*

As citizens of the Kingdom, you also have the spiritual blessing of the new birth, the Holy Spirit in you. In fact, this new covenant *"is superior to the old one, since the new covenant is established on better promises"* (Hebrews 8:6b).

> *Praise be to the God and Father of our Lord Jesus Christ, who has blessed us in the heavenly realms with every spiritual blessing in Christ.*
>
> *—Ephesians 1:3*

So, in the same way that Joseph prospered because he had the blessing of God, you should also expect to prosper because you also have the blessing of God.

What Determines Promotion?

However, it is true that you and I know a lot of people who have this blessing, and yet we don't see prosperity in their lives.

Why is that?

As spiritual scientists, we need to dig a little deeper into the facts for clues.

> *The Lord was with Joseph so that he prospered, and he lived in the house of his Egyptian master. When his master saw that the Lord was with him and that the Lord gave him success in everything he did, Joseph found favor in his eyes and became his attendant. Potiphar put him in charge of his household, and he entrusted to his care everything he owned.*
>
> —Genesis 39:2-4

Notice what happened after Potiphar saw that the Lord was with Joseph. The Scripture says, *"Potiphar put him in charge."* In other words, Joseph was promoted.

When we think about someone getting a promotion, the first thing that comes to mind is often a raise. Typically, we think a promotion means more money. But that's not how it really works.

What actually happens when someone is promoted is that they are promoted into more responsibility. And as the responsibility gets bigger, the paychecks get bigger.

The world pays people to handle responsibility and take authority.

Let's consider the word *responsibility*. The root meaning is to "respond with" your ability.[4] There is an assignment—a task, a problem to fix—and you respond with your ability to that task to accomplish it.

What Potiphar saw in Joseph was his response to his assignment and the way he carried that responsibility.

What kind of responsibility was Joseph handling? He was a

slave in Potiphar's house. He was cleaning toilets.

That's what Potiphar saw: "Those are the cleanest toilets I've ever seen in my life! That guy did the best job on a menial task that I've ever seen anyone do!"

But what if you don't want to be good at menial tasks? What if your goal is to be a ruler?

Remember, everyone starts someplace. And from there, it becomes a matter of responding to these tasks and handling them with integrity. How you handle your responsibilities is what determines your promotion.

This is something we need to hear more about in our culture. We see people trying to market themselves into new positions all the time without first demonstrating any character. But it just doesn't work that way.

What Else Could Go Wrong?

As Joseph's story continues, Potiphar saw that the Lord was with Joseph, and he placed him in charge of his entire household and possessions. And as a result of his promotion, *"the Lord blessed the household of the Egyptian because of Joseph"* (Genesis 39:5b).

But that's not the end of the story. There was another complication for Joseph.

> *Now Joseph was well-built and handsome, and after a while his master's wife took notice of Joseph and said, "Come to bed with me!"*
>
> —Genesis 39:6b-7

Joseph immediately refused her advances. He told her:

> *"No one is greater in this house than I am. My master has withheld nothing from me except you, because you are his wife. How then could I do such a wicked thing and sin against God?"*
>
> —Genesis 39:9

Angered and perhaps embarrassed by his rejection, Potiphar's wife accused Joseph of attempted rape.

> *When his master heard the story his wife told him, saying, "This is how your slave treated me," he burned with anger.*

> *Joseph's master took him and put him in prison, the place where the king's prisoners were confined.*
>
> —Genesis 39:19-20a

Once again, Joseph found himself in an impossible situation. But again, we see the blessing of Abraham at work in Joseph's life. The Lord was with Joseph in prison, and before long he was running the entire prison.

> *But while Joseph was there in the prison, the Lord was with him; he showed him kindness and granted him favor in the eyes of the prison warden. So, the warden put Joseph in charge of all those held in the prison, and he was made responsible for all that was done there. The warden paid no attention to anything under Joseph's care, because the Lord was with Joseph and gave him success in whatever he did.*
>
> —Genesis 39:20b-23

In prison, Joseph continued doing the same thing he did in Potiphar's house—the one thing that any of us can do that will produce favor everywhere we go—he handled his responsibilities with excellence.

Ask any business owner how they feel about those employees

who care about the prosperity of their business and actually work hard for its success. If you will do everything with your ability to help your boss succeed and prosper, you will be recognized and have favor—it's guaranteed!

Joseph was in prison. No one knew him there. No one except God. But soon, the prison warden began to see the success the Lord gave Joseph in everything he did.

So, the prison warden promoted Joseph and gave him the responsibility for the other prisoners and all the daily prison operations.

This was the same as at Potiphar's house. No matter where Joseph found himself, he was serving the Lord with his entire heart and handling his responsibilities faithfully with God's help—and he was prospering unto the Lord.

You may be working in a dark place right now. You may not see any glory there. But that just means you need to brighten it up! You can always bring light, no matter where you are.

As it happened, Pharaoh threw two of his employees, a cupbearer and a baker, into prison. They were not there very long before they met Joseph, because he was in charge of the prison.

Later they both had dreams, then they went to Joseph and shared their dreams with him, because they had heard he could interpret dreams.

And Joseph did so.

He told the cupbearer that his dream meant that he would soon return to service in the king's court.

And he told the baker that his dream meant that he would soon be executed.

In both cases, that was what happened.

The cupbearer went back to work in Pharaoh's court, and it seemed he had forgotten all about Joseph—until two years later when the day came that Pharaoh himself had a very upsetting dream, and none of his magicians or wise men were able to interpret it for him.

CHAPTER
FOUR

SUDDEN
PROMOTION

In the morning his mind was troubled, so he sent for all the magicians and wise men of Egypt. Pharaoh told them his dreams, but no one could interpret them for him.

Then the chief cupbearer said to Pharaoh, "Today I am reminded of my shortcomings. Pharaoh was once angry with his servants, and he imprisoned me and the chief baker in the house of the captain of the guard. Each of us had a dream the same night, and each dream had a meaning of its own. Now a young Hebrew was there with us, a servant of the captain of the guard. We told him our dreams, and he interpreted them for us, giving each man the interpretation of his dream. And things turned out exactly as he interpreted them to us: I was restored to my position, and the other man was impaled."

So Pharaoh sent for Joseph, and he was quickly brought from the dungeon. When he had shaved and changed his clothes, he came before Pharaoh.

Pharaoh said to Joseph, "I had a dream, and no one can interpret it. But I have heard it said of you that when you hear a dream you can interpret it."

"I cannot do it," Joseph replied to Pharaoh, "but God will give Pharaoh the answer he desires."

—Genesis 41:8-16

Often, what looks like a sudden promotion was not really so sudden after all.

To those in Pharaoh's court, Joseph's promotion must have seemed extraordinary. One day Joseph was in prison and without hope—and the next day he was standing in front of the throne with a fresh shave and new clothes as Pharaoh appointed him as acting CEO of Egypt.

Except in the movies, it doesn't happen that way. In real life, promotion begins underground, out of sight, when no one knows your name.

Because underground is where your loyalty, your faithfulness, and your integrity are tested.

Even though everything may be stacked against you—the dysfunction in your family life, the disloyalty you've faced, the pain and helplessness and hopelessness you've experienced— if you handle things with a mindset of excellence, the living God sees you. And He knows your name.

Pharaoh said to Joseph, "*I have heard it said of you....*"

If someone called your employer today for a reference, what would be said of you?

"I have heard you clean toilets really well."

Some people discount menial tasks. They don't understand that it's in the menial tasks that they will develop an attitude of excellence. It is faithfulness in the little things that develops integrity.

God knows where you are and what you do. He knows your name. You don't have to market yourself out of an impossible situation. You just have to serve the living God with your entire heart and know that He can bring you out—*and He will bring you out!*

God Is in the Promotion Business

Years ago, I was in Albania when God spoke to me about going to the nations. "I'm sending you to the nations to share my financial covenant of blessing," He told me. "And wherever you go, I'll pay for it."

At the time, I wondered what this meant. Was I to begin traveling all the time to various places around world?

But when we got home, I began to feel a stirring toward television, although we knew nothing about television. (And we weren't sure we wanted to know more.)

Then Drenda was having lunch with a couple of ladies, and one of them asked her, "Are you doing television yet?"

Isn't that interesting? We were nobodies. No one knew us. And this was the first time Drenda had met this lady.

Then the lady said, "Well, when you're ready, call this guy." She handed Drenda a slip of paper with a name and an email address.

Drenda and I were at our desks in the office later on when she found that slip of paper in her purse. "I'm going to email this guy," she said. "You know, just to see what's out there."

So, she emailed this guy, and he invited us to the NRB's (National Religious Broadcasters) national event in Nashville. He wanted to meet with us and talk about television. He asked us to come to his penthouse suite at the Gaylord Hotel in Nashville.

I bought a new suit, and we went to Nashville. Television was new territory for us, and I was a little nervous. We walked back and forth in front of the door for a few minutes before I finally knocked on the door.

We were ushered into the suite where seven people in suits were sitting in a semi-circle around two chairs.

We made ourselves as comfortable as possible, and they started asking us about television. Why did we want to do television? What made us think we could do television?

All we could do was talk about the passion we have for sharing the Kingdom message. That's all we had. We didn't know anything about television.

But afterward, the guy told us he wanted to explore the possibility of doing television with us and wanted to come out to our home.

We knew his name, but we didn't really know who he was. After he flew in to meet with us and sat us down, he said, "Now, in case you don't know about me, I do Joel Osteen's television broadcast. I do Joyce's broadcast." And he listed a few other ministries he was also working with.

As we talked that afternoon, I kept thinking to myself, "How did this guy end up here, at the end of our gravel road in the middle of nowhere? How did this happen?"

God is in the business of sudden promotion. We can safely put our trust in Him—no matter how impossible it may seem.

The day came, all of a sudden, when people at home turned on their television sets, and there were Gary and Drenda. And they wondered, "Where did they come from? How did this happen?"

Well, it happened back in Albania. It happened at lunch. It happened in Nashville. And then there was a day when circumstances and God came together and brought us to a new place of destiny.

Pharaoh said to Joseph, "*I have heard it said of you....*"

> *A good name is more desirable than great riches; to be esteemed is better than silver or gold.*
> —Proverbs 22:1

Overflowing Piles of Grain

So, Pharaoh put his ring on Joseph's finger—the signet ring that gave Joseph the same authority that Pharaoh had. He put a gold chain around his neck. And he put him in charge of the whole land of Egypt.

Can you guess what happened next?

Remember, Joseph had the covenant. He had the promises. He had the blessing.

Yes, once again, Joseph had great success! The Lord prospered everything he did—and then his blessing overflowed into all of Egypt as well!

> *And Joseph went out from Pharaoh's presence and traveled throughout Egypt. During the seven years of abundance the land produced plentifully. Joseph collected all the food produced in those seven years of abundance in Egypt and stored it in the cities. In each city he put the food grown in the fields surrounding it. Joseph stored up huge quantities of grain, like the sand of the sea; it was so much that he stopped keeping records because it was beyond measure.*
>
> —Genesis 41:46b-49

Egypt was then the wealthiest nation on the earth, and they had so much grain they couldn't even store it all. If you were speculating in commodities that year, that would have been a great investment!

Then seven years later when the severe famine hit, Egypt was ready. As surrounding nations crashed and burned, and their people were dying of starvation, Egypt shone like a beacon of light.

> *The seven years of abundance in Egypt came to an end, and the seven years of famine began, just as Joseph had said. There was famine in all the other lands, but in the whole land of Egypt there was food. When all Egypt began to feel the famine, the people cried to Pharaoh for food. Then Pharaoh told all the Egyptians, "Go to Joseph and do what he tells you."*

> *When the famine had spread over the whole country, Joseph opened all the storehouses and sold grain to the Egyptians, for the famine was severe throughout Egypt. And all the world came to Egypt to buy grain from Joseph, because the famine was severe everywhere.*

> —Genesis 41:53-57

THE GRAIN PILE PRINCIPLE

People from all nations started coming to Egypt to get the grain they needed to survive.

This is the blessing of the Lord—it's what I call the "Grain Pile Principle"—and it's amazing!

We saw it work in slavery.
We saw it work in prison.
We saw it work in Egypt.

The blessing of the Lord works wherever you are! It produces results! And it brings change! God wants to bless and prosper you so that you can bless your neighbor, your city, your nation, and even the whole world. And this blessing starts with *you*.

My friend, this is your destiny. I call this the Grain Pile Principle because this is how your life should work. I want you to picture a big pile of grain in your mind. This is what your life is supposed to look like—piles and piles and piles of grain!

> *Give, and it will be given to you. A good measure, pressed down, shaken together and running over, will be poured into your lap. For with the measure you use, it will be measured to you.*
>
> —Luke 6:38

Then your life becomes a light for someone else. They see the difference in you. They see you have peace. They see you are successful and prospering.

And then you can tell them the good news of the promises of God. That's what the word "Gospel" means—good news! You share this good news and invite them to join you in the covenant of Abraham and the blessing of God!

This Is Your Inheritance!

So, why aren't more believers experiencing this overflowing blessing and enjoying these overflowing piles of grain?

One reason is that many people don't know about the promises of God. They don't know who they are in Christ. They don't know about the blessing. They don't understand the ways things work in the Kingdom of God.

Another reason is that they're not reaching for the blessing. They don't believe the promises are for them. They don't realize that every promise is "yes" in Christ (2 Corinthians 1:20) and that no begging is required! They don't understand that they already have every single promise in the Bible—and so now it's just a matter of getting their thinking straight.

Do not conform to the pattern of this world, but be transformed by the renewing of your mind.

—Romans 12:2a

A third reason may be because they are still locked in prison. They are listening to the devil, the accuser of the brethren, who does not want them to find out who they really are. So, they continue to struggle with guilt and condemnation. They don't know that God sent Jesus to bring them out of their prison and set them free as a son or daughter of God.

For the accuser of our brothers and sisters, who accuses them before our God day and night, has been hurled down.

—Revelation 12:10b

I wrote this book with one purpose in mind: I want to wake you up!

Because you need to know who you are. I want you to know that right now you have the blessing of God on your life! You have the promises of God! You can do all things through Christ who strengthens you, and whatever you put your hand to will prosper!

What if you've made some mistakes? Well, we all have. That's why Jesus died on the cross. Jesus paid for our mistakes, and He has set us free from guilt!

So now in Him, you are forgiven and have every right to all of the promises because you have been grafted into the lineage and blessing of Abraham. Jesus Himself has *"redeemed us in order that the blessing given to Abraham might come to the Gentiles"* (Galatians 3:14a).

That means everything you read in Deuteronomy 28 belongs to you—and every promise is yours!

You have the same promises that Joseph had, you have the same blessing, and you have the spiritual blessing through Jesus Christ. You've been born again! Not only do you have the blessing of Abraham, but you also have the blessing of being a son or a daughter of the house. This means you have the inheritance—the spiritual life of God, the Holy Spirit dwelling within you, and the blessing of Abraham. All of it is yours!

You are to be a lender, not a borrower! You ought to have more than enough, so that you can be generous on every occasion! You should anticipate that God will do mighty and miraculous things in your life! And you should expect to experience amazing divine promotions until you reach the place of destiny that God has ordained you for!

Your mind should be on tilt right now.

God Has a Future for You!

How is this possible? Think about Joseph. How was it possible for him?

He was a young man sold into slavery. He was a slave accused of raping an Egyptian military captain's wife and was sentenced to life in prison.

So, why was Joseph put in charge of all of Egypt?

The Lord was with him. He had the blessing and promises of God. This went all the way back to his great-grandfather, Abraham, who made a covenant with God. Joseph was in the lineage of Abraham, and so this gave God access to bring His influence into Joseph's life.

Joseph prospered because the Lord brought Him success.

But that's not why he was promoted. Time after time, he was promoted based solely on the excellence of his work. The Egyptian officer, the prison warden, and Pharaoh had each observed that there was something different about him.

Joseph knew who he was. He had seen himself ruling since he was a young boy. He knew he was innocent concerning Potiphar's wife. He knew he was coming out of that prison. He knew He had the blessing of God and the promises of God. And so Joseph put his confidence in God.

It's the same for you. God has a future for you. Even if it looks impossible for you, it's possible with God.

You just need to understand the process.

CHAPTER
FIVE

THE
GRAIN PILE
PROCESS

Perhaps the title of this book should have been *The Grain Pile Process,* because this is a process. Picture Joseph's overflowing piles of grain. How did that grain get there?

There was a process.

And it's important that we understand each step of this process if we are to enjoy the blessings and promises of God.

STEP ONE: Blessing

Everything starts with the blessing of God. So, our first step is to understand the covenant of blessing that God established with Abraham and his descendants.

You need to know who God is, who you are, and who you are called to be. It's also important to know what God has promised you, because these promises will dictate your future.

> *The Lord will open the heavens, the storehouse of his bounty, to send rain on your land in season and to bless all the work of your hands. You will lend to many nations but will borrow from none. The Lord will make you the head, not the tail. If you pay attention to the commands*

of the Lord your God that I give you this day and carefully follow them, you will always be at the top, never at the bottom.

—Deuteronomy 28:12-13

But if you don't know that you already have the promise of God's blessing, then you have nothing to hold on to. And the life you live will be identical to that of any unbeliever who does not have the promises.

You are a descendant of Abraham—whether by your physical lineage or by being grafted in through Christ—and so you share in the covenant of blessing. This means God will bless all the work of your hands. So, you have a choice: You can choose to grow three tomato plants under the blessing, or you can grow 50,000 tomato plants under the blessing. It's up to you. It's your legal right. It is who you are. The blessing is yours.

STEP TWO: Preparation

You will only prepare for where you think you're going. We have no reason to reach for things we do not see.

So, the second step in this process is preparation. Every

day, we are each preparing *for* something—to receive, to apprehend, to occupy, or to take hold of something—and what we prepare for will depend upon the future we see.

The promises of God offer us a picture of something in the future. They show us who we are and what we will do. If we believe this picture—and we expect these benefits—it will change how we act. It will cause us to prepare.

What you are preparing for will give you insight into what you believe about yourself.

For example, if you believe you are going to be a concert violinist, you will probably practice the violin. Or if you have no desire to practice—or you don't think it's possible for you to become a concert violinist—you may not even pick up the instrument.

Preparation is about moving toward the promise—the picture—of where you see yourself headed. If you're wasting time watching 20 hours of television every week, then you believe you're going nowhere because you believe you're a nowhere person.

Imagine I hand you a check for $500. Would you have $500

CHAPTER FIVE: THE GRAIN PILE PROCESS

at that moment? No, not quite. What you would have in your hand is a piece of paper. It's a promise. We call it a promissory note. But you can't just take that piece of paper to a store and spend it. If you want to enjoy the benefit of it, you first have to go to the bank and cash it.

So, the promise causes you to change your direction. First, you go to the bank. Then, you go and spend the money. You have to enact the process of banking if you wish to benefit from the promise.

In the same way, if you believe the promises of God, it will change the way you act.

A Person of Excellence

So, ask yourself: What am I envisioning right now? What am I preparing to do? What am I rehearsing? What am I practicing? What promise fills my thoughts with hope?

This matters because it is an indication of who you think you are. You will only prepare for the future that you believe is yours.

And this preparation begins before anyone knows your name.

We know the promises of God are true—the Bible says it is impossible for God to lie (Hebrews 6:18). So, why aren't more people enjoying the benefits and blessings of the promises of God?

I see two possible reasons—either they don't know what God has promised or they simply don't believe it.

We saw that Joseph believed the promises of God. He had a dream. He knew he was a leader. He did not believe he would stay in that prison. He practiced who he was in Potiphar's house. He practiced who he was in prison. He was faithful over the smallest details of every menial task because his confidence was in God.

Joseph wasn't a man trying to do excellent things; He was a man of excellence. What you believe about yourself is what you do.

This is why we see Joseph imprisoned in a dungeon with a life sentence one day, and the next day, he has a fresh shave, clean clothes, and is standing before Pharaoh being put in charge of the whole country.

It looked like sudden promotion to the people who saw him arrive at the king's court in chains, but it wasn't sudden—not to God. Joseph had been faithful. Joseph was ready. His promotion came as preparation and revelation met opportunity.

One of the biggest misconceptions that I see among Christians is that they think God waved some kind of magical spiritual wand over Joseph's life, and that is what caused him to prosper. They think that success happened *to* Joseph instead of *through* him.

I have known many Christians in financial dysfunction because they were able to quote all the promises, but they didn't follow the process. They were still waiting for a magical spiritual wand.

But Joseph was successful because he passed the faithfulness test. Potiphar saw that God was with him. Pharaoh saw that God was with him.

STEP THREE: Revelation

Pharaoh had a troubling dream. There would be seven years of great abundance coming throughout the land of Egypt, and then seven years of severe famine would follow them. This famine would ravage the land, and all the abundance in Egypt would be forgotten.

The first step of revelation is discernment. Joseph properly interpreted Pharaoh's dream, and then he discerned the problem.

> *The reason the dream was given to Pharaoh in two forms is that the matter has been firmly decided by God, and God will do it soon.*
>
> —Genesis 41:32

Once Joseph knew what was going to happen, he was able to give Pharaoh the solution.

> *And now let Pharaoh look for a discerning and wise man and put him in charge of the land of Egypt. Let Pharaoh appoint commissioners over the land to take a fifth of the harvest of Egypt during the seven years of abundance.*

They should collect all the food of these good years that are coming and store up the grain under the authority of Pharaoh, to be kept in the cities for food. This food should be held in reserve for the country, to be used during the seven years of famine that will come upon Egypt, so that the country may not be ruined by the famine.

—Genesis 41:33-36

Unlike many employees, Joseph was not a complainer or a grumbler. Instead, he said, "I have a solution for this."

He discerned not only the problem, but he also discerned a solution to fix it—and he discerned the plan to administrate it. No wonder he prospered!

This should be you, if the Spirit of God is in you. You should prosper in everything you put your hand to.

But are you just going to sit there and drink lemonade as you wait for it to show up? Absolutely not! You're going to enact revelation.

God is going to give you revelation because the Spirit of God is in you. Anyone can see the problem, but Joseph prospered because he knew how to walk out the problem with a plan and a solution.

So, how do you do this? How do you get revelation? How do you get a plan? How do you gain wisdom?

> *The beginning of wisdom is this: Get wisdom. Though it cost all you have, get understanding.*
>
> —Proverbs 4:7

Wisdom begins when you realize that you don't know it all. Wisdom comes when you recognize that you don't have it all together—because you don't. The beginning of wisdom is when you lay aside your pride and look to God.

> *If any of you lacks wisdom, you should ask God, who gives generously to all without finding fault, and it will be given to you.*
>
> —James 1:5

The Word of God

The first way to get wisdom is to look in the written Word of God. It is God's instruction manual.

Have you ever attempted to put something together—a bookcase, a bicycle, a toy—and then when you got done there was a part left over because you didn't read the instructions carefully? And then you had to tear it all apart and rebuild it? That happens to me all the time.

The Bible is filled with God's instructions for how life is supposed to work. This piece goes here, that piece goes there. Join A to B here. You just need to follow the directions.

From time to time, someone will come to me as their pastor. They tell me they're praying about a particular person and want to know if I think it might be God's will for them to get married.

"Is this person a Christian?" I'll ask. "Do they come to church?"

Sometimes they say, "No."

"Well, stop praying," I tell them. "I already know that God does not want you to marry that person at this time. The Bible says, *Do not be yoked together with unbelievers*" (2 Corinthians 6:14a).

If we want God's wisdom, sometimes we just need to open our Bibles.

A *Rhema* Word

A second way you can gain wisdom is with the revealed word of God—a *Rhema*.

At times, we need a specific revelation because the Bible doesn't tell us who to marry, if we should sell our stock, or if we should move to Oklahoma. We need to be led by the Holy Spirit.

> *For those who are led by the Spirit of God are the children of God.*
>
> —Romans 8:14

As Jesus was about to leave the earth, He told His disciples that the Holy Spirit would come to give them revelation and teach them everything they needed to know.

> *"All this I have spoken while still with you. But the Advocate, the Holy Spirit, whom the Father will send in my name, will teach you all things and will remind you of everything I have said to you."*
>
> —John 14:25-26

If Jesus said the Holy Spirit would "teach you all things," would you assume that would encompass any situation that you might encounter? Could you assume that God might possibly have an answer for any situation you will face? And if you have the Holy Spirit in your life, could you expect to have access to all that knowledge?

> *Trust in the Lord with all your heart and lean not on your own understanding; in all your ways submit to him, and he will make your paths straight.*
> —Proverbs 3:5-6

We just need to listen to God. Of course, we don't always do that, do we? I don't always do it. But then we find ourselves heading down paths we regret—and we wish we would have asked.

Fortunately, we can ask Him for wisdom at any time. There are nine gifts of the Holy Spirit listed in 1 Corinthians 12:4-10. They have not passed away. Two of them—the Word of Knowledge and the Word of Wisdom (revelation concerning direction) always come in handy.

> *There are different kinds of gifts, but the same Spirit distributes them. To one there is given through the Spirit*

a message of wisdom, to another a message of knowledge by means of the same Spirit.

—1 Corinthians 12:4, 8

You may not be aware of this, but you have all nine of these spiritual gifts. We hear people say that they have this gift or that gift, but if they truly have the Holy Spirit, then they have all nine gifts—because the Holy Spirit in them has all nine gifts.

If we were limited and could not operate in all of the gifts, then Paul would not have told us to eagerly desire these spiritual gifts (1 Corinthians 14:1). All the gifts of the Holy Spirit are there in you and for you if you need them.

Wise Counsel

A third way you can gain wisdom is through wise counsel. God can use other people in your life—family, friends, pastors, and those whom He has put in authority over you— to speak to you.

For lack of guidance a nation falls, but victory is won through many advisers.

—Proverbs 11:14

It's also worth mentioning that there are times when we don't need more revelation. We just need to be obedient to what we already know.

So, if you need wisdom, you may wish to ask yourself if you have done the last thing God told you to do. It's always important to be diligent to do what we already know to do.

STEP FOUR: Administration

One morning a few years ago, I was praying, and God said to me, "I'm going to tell you why a lot of My people do not enjoy the promises."

I've observed that many people can quote the promises, but they never see the blessing in their lives. We all fail in this at times, but the bottom line is that there's a piece missing.

God led me to the eleventh chapter of Hebrews—the "Hall of Fame" for faith—with its list of people *who through faith conquered kingdoms, administered justice, and gained what was promised"* (Hebrews 11:33a).

He showed me the entire process in this one sentence.

These people had the promise, and then they acted by faith—conquering, administering, and then finally gaining the promise.

Revelation is an awesome thing. Joseph discerned not only the dream but also the situation. After he had explained to Pharaoh what was going to happen, he then presented the plan that God had given him.

What if Joseph had stopped there? What if he had the revelation of the dream and a revelation of the plan, but then the plan was never enacted or administrated?

> *The plan seemed good to Pharaoh and to all his officials. So Pharaoh asked them, "Can we find anyone like this man, one in whom is the spirit of God?"*
>
> *Then Pharaoh said to Joseph, "Since God has made all this known to you, there is no one so discerning and wise as you. You shall be in charge of my palace, and all my people are to submit to your orders."*
>
> —Genesis 41:37-40a

Joseph's plan seemed good to Pharaoh and to all of his officials, and they felt he was the right man to execute the plan.

So, Joseph was put in charge of the whole operation.

What was Joseph's secret for success here? First, he discerned the situation. Then he solved the problem by developing a plan, and then he developed a way to administrate the plan. So it was in this process that we see God gave Joseph this success.

Perhaps anyone could have seen the problem. But in this case, God gave Joseph discernment. He gave him wisdom. He gave him a solution. And He gave him a plan for administering that solution. And in this, Pharaoh saw that the Lord was with Joseph.

How Authority Works

> *So Pharaoh said to Joseph, "I hereby put you in charge of the whole land of Egypt." Then Pharaoh took his signet ring from his finger and put it on Joseph's finger.*
> —Genesis 41:41-42a

Why did Pharaoh give Joseph his ring? Because it was a symbol of the authority he had bestowed upon Joseph.

If you going to administrate something, you must have the authority to do it.

This also means you have to know how authority operates. If you do not know how to submit to authority, there is no way you will be able to successfully manage others.

You may not like your boss. You may hate him. He may be crummy, or she may be mean. But God is giving you an opportunity to be the light where you are right now and a chance to practice submitting to your boss, to your leaders, to your parents, to your pastors, or to whoever He puts in your life.

God has you where you are for you to practice submitting to authorities, so that someday you can rule with authority.

This kind of practice is particularly important for you as a follower of Jesus Christ. You need to understand authority because you have been given the authority to carry out the plan of salvation.

> *Then Jesus came to them and said, "All authority in heaven and on earth has been given to me. Therefore go and make disciples of all nations...."*
> —Matthew 28:18-19

Before Jesus paid the price for mankind on the cross, the earth had been under the dominion of Satan. But when Jesus came out of the grave, He received all authority in the heavens and the earth realm. And now He sends out His followers with this same authority: "*Therefore go and make disciples of all nations.*"

In other words, you have been given the authority to administrate heaven on Earth. Yes, you have been given a position of authority in the government of God! You are seated with Christ in heavenly places. You have been given both the signet ring and the blessing!

Accessing the Wisdom of God

Ultimately, Joseph's success stemmed from the lineage of Abraham, and Jesus Christ came from this same root.

> *A shoot will come up from the stump of Jesse; from his roots a Branch will bear fruit. The Spirit of the Lord will rest on him—the Spirit of wisdom and of understanding, the Spirit of counsel and of might, the Spirit of the knowledge and fear of the Lord— and he will delight in the fear of the Lord.*
> —Isaiah 11:1-3a

This means you have access to the Spirit of God! The same Holy Spirit that rested upon Jesus dwells in you—because you are the temple of the Holy Spirit. This means you now have access to this same knowledge, understanding (which is discernment), counsel, and wisdom.

> *By wisdom a house is built, and through understanding it is established; through knowledge its rooms are filled with rare and beautiful treasures.*
>
> —Proverbs 24:3-4

We can define wisdom as the application of experience, knowledge, and good judgment. But what if you don't have experience? What if you don't have knowledge? God has plenty of both!

The Lord will make it possible for you to make judgments beyond your natural ability and give you discernment past your natural ability.

One of the reasons we need wisdom is because the real problem is often hidden. You have to be able to see past the surface.

Everyone can see the result of the problem, but to solve it, you have to find the root of the problem. And you need the Holy

Spirit to help you discern the problem, bring a solution for it, and then administrate it.

This is how God gave Joseph success. And this is how He will give you success.

God did not wave a magical spiritual wand over Joseph. Joseph was successful because when he was in charge, Potiphar didn't have to worry about a thing. The prison warden didn't have to worry about a thing—because when Joseph was there to discern and administrate, everything ran smoothly.

You have access to this same ability—because the Holy Spirit in you has this ability. Even if you don't have it personally, God will connect you with people who have what you need.

So, you need to start operating with the complete picture. You have to start thinking bigger. You have to reset your default. You have been created to solve problems. The Holy Spirit in you is bigger than you give Him credit for, because with Him, you can do all things through Christ! (Philippians 4:13).

So often, people don't reach for this because they don't understand the blessing. They don't know who they are in Christ. They don't know how to hear the plans of God or how to walk them out. They're going to heaven, but they are only looking at life in the earth realm. They're still enslaved in their minds.

As I mentioned earlier, Drenda and I were in serious debt for nine long, hard years. It was really bad. We didn't have much, and what we had was broken. We had borrowed from our parents. We had IRS liens. I was having panic attacks and was on antidepressants. And we didn't know how to get free.

At the time, we were Christians. We loved God. We went to church. But we didn't know what we know today. We did not understand the process or how to enact the process. Sure, we could quote a Scripture, but we didn't know how to take a Scripture, walk it out, and bring it into reality.

Then one night, I had a dream to start a company—which became the solution to our poverty problem.

Of course, a lot of people have dreams. As a pastor, I hear it all the time. "God told me to do this, to start that." But without the process, nothing happens. Too many people have the mentality that God is going to do it in spite of them. First, we have the process—and then God meets us in the process.

Engaging the Process

Our world is in trouble right now, and everyone is looking for answers. They're in a famine, fighting for life in a land that is totally barren. They are looking for someone with a grain pile.

You have a grain pile, so that's going to stand out. You have a great marriage, and that is going to stand out. Your kids are obedient, and that is going to stand out. You have peace. You're living without debt. You're kind. You're generous. And so not only will all of this stand out but God also wants your grain pile to stand out!

But to accumulate a grain pile requires a plan. We need to understand the process, and we need to walk it out. Engaging the process is at the heart of the Grain Pile Principle. Administering the plan is where most people miss it.

People come to me all the time as their pastor and tell me that God gave them a vision to start a business. Then five years later, I check in with them and learn nothing has changed.

What happened to the dream? What happened to the plan? Sure, they had the revelation. They heard from God. They might have had a plan. But they never administrated it. They never walked it out.

Why not? Because that's the hard part. Revelation is easy. Putting a plan together is simple. But administration is when it gets hard. That's when you've got to get in there and manage it and make it happen.

And that's when people quit. They think God is going to administrate the plan for them.

But there is some good news—God will never give you a plan that you can't administrate!

Sure, you'll have to stretch a little, but that's all right. Because the world only pays big money for big problem solvers.

Let's say you are believing God for a million dollars. This is likely to stretch you because getting a million dollars will require solving some big problems.

But for some people, the first problem they have to solve is how to get up in the morning and get to work on time. Everyone has to start somewhere. You have to begin by administrating what you have in your hands right now. How do you expect to manage a company of two million employees if you can't get to work on time? Or if your car is a trash pile?

Everyone needs to learn how to administrate—because you will never occupy what you do not administrate. So, administration begins with the little things. This is something you should be practicing now. It may not matter to you that your bed is not made or that your house is a mess because nobody will see it. But you see it. And this gives you the chance to practice cleaning and organizing—because someday, you'll get to organize and clean something much bigger.

STEP FIVE: Harvest

The great famine lasted seven years. Nations were devastated, and people died. But in Egypt, we find Joseph stored up huge quantities of grain —like the sand of the sea— so much grain, in fact, that they stopped keeping records because it was beyond measure.

On one hand, there was famine, death, and destruction. On the other, there was Egypt with so much provision—so many piles of grain—that they couldn't even count it all. That's why I call this the Grain Pile Principle. This is the picture we should have in our minds.

Why are all those grain piles there? Because of the blessing.

Potiphar's house was blessed because Joseph was blessed—and the blessing of the Lord came on Potiphar's house because Joseph was there. The prison was blessed because Joseph was there. And Egypt was prospering because it was under Joseph's authority; and there was so much grain that it couldn't be counted.

In a famine, grain is life—and Joseph held the key to the grain piles.

This should be you. This should be your life. You should have huge piles of grain.

These days, we live in a world that is hurting and being ripped apart. It is in strife and dysfunction, in poverty, sickness, and disease. And there are no answers out there.

In this famine, there is only one group of people—the body of Christ—that holds the key to the grain piles.

So, the world has to come to us. As a member of the body of Christ, through the proclamation of what Jesus has done for you, you become the dispenser of the grain pile that offers life.

You have the blessing—blessing beyond the blessing—of Abraham. You have life in Christ. You've been adopted into the family of God as a son or daughter of the house, and your inheritance is the entire Kingdom! Your life is supposed to be the grain pile!

Ruling and Reigning in Life

Joseph, in the lineage of Abraham, was in a dungeon when he came out suddenly to run the entire nation of Egypt.

He was dressed in robes of fine linen with a gold chain around his neck. He rode in a chariot as Pharaoh's second-in-command, and all the people shouted before him, "Make way!" He was in charge of the whole land of Egypt (Genesis 41:42-43).

Jesus, also in the lineage of Abraham, was in the tomb three days; and then He came out suddenly at the right hand of the Father to rule over the entire earth realm.

He captured back what Satan had captured through Adam's disobedience—the earth realm. Now, the poverty, famine, and dysfunction of the earth realm no longer have a hold on you.

Now, you wear a gold necklace and fine linen. You have been made royalty. *"The blessing of the Lord brings wealth, without painful toil for it"* (Proverbs 10:22).

Now, as the body of Christ, the demons squeal and make way as we move through the earth on our mission to administrate salvation to the planet and set the captives free!

> *And these signs will accompany those who believe: In my name they will drive out demons; they will speak in new tongues; they will pick up snakes with their hands; and when they drink deadly poison, it will not hurt them at all; they will place their hands on sick people, and they will get well.*
>
> —Mark 16:17-18

When the famine began to get really intense in Egypt, the people came to Pharaoh and said, "We need grain! We must have grain!" Then Pharaoh said, "Go to Joseph and do whatever he says."

My friend, it's time to take your eyes off that person you were in prison, even if you think you deserved to be there. Even if your dysfunction, your background, your family problems, or the mistakes you've made are the most hideous things you can imagine—they just don't matter anymore.

You were never supposed to stay in prison. Like Joseph, you were created to be riding on a chariot, ruling and reigning in life, administrating the plan of God!

So, you need to stop looking at that prison cell—and get your eyes on who you were created to be! In the same way that God brought Joseph out of that mess and set him in that place of royalty, He has already done the same for you!

> *And God raised us up with Christ and seated us with him*
> *in the heavenly realms in Christ Jesus.*
>
> —Ephesians 2:6

You may know that Drenda and I lived in Tulsa for a few years. I was out jogging one day, and God said to me, "Move to Ohio."

My first thought was, *Are you kidding?*

The problem was that the whole economy of Tulsa was based on oil—and at the time, oil was crashing big time. One-third of the houses in Tulsa were on the market. There was not a U-Haul trailer available in the entire city.

This was not the perfect time for us to sell. Our house was worth less than we owed on it. Real estate had crashed. But God said to move.

Since our bank held the mortgage, I went in to see what could be done because we were upside down.

When I walked in, there was a tall stack of papers on the woman's desk. We started talking, and she said, "Listen, one thing I don't want is another foreclosure." She pointed to the stack of papers. "That's what all these are."

She looked at me for a moment. "I'll tell you what I will do," she said. "You sell the house for whatever it appraisees for, and we'll call it even. I'll give you six months to sell it, and you can just pay half of the house payment during those six months. Sell the house, and we're fine."

Praise God! That was amazing news! We were pretty happy about that.

So, we signed up with a real estate company. Over the next five months, not one person called. Not one person came by.

Believe me, we started praying about this. We had to get a

deal done in six months or they would withdraw their offer. I would have to pay back the other half of the payments that I made (I had already spent that money). And we would still be upside down on the house.

Then, we were four weeks away. "God," we prayed, "You told us to move. What should we do?" He told us to call the real estate company and get out of the contract.

So, I called. "You guys haven't done a thing for us," I said. "Let us take over." And they said, "Okay."

We prayed over the house, and Drenda orchestrated the plan God gave her. We ran one ad in the newspaper, put some balloons out front, and had an open house. We were three weeks away from the deadline.

A lady came to the open house and said she wanted to buy the house. Praise God! But these were not the days of "no verification" loans. It didn't matter what your credit rating was—they had to mail out verifications to employers and creditors and then wait for them to come back. We knew it could take a month to process the loan, and we had a little over two weeks.

But not only did this lady want the house, she also had cash.

So, we went into the bank and told the lady we had a cash buyer. Her mouth dropped open, and she slammed her palms on the table. "Where on Earth did you find a buyer?" she asked.

"We didn't," I told her. "God did."

The Grain Pile Life

I hope this look at the life of Joseph has helped you understand that you can prosper even if you find yourself, like him, in the midst of an impossible situation, surrounded by ungodly people who know nothing about God.

You have been given the blessing and promise of God. You have been given a position. You've been adopted into the family as a son or daughter of God, and you have been given an amazing inheritance—the entire Kingdom.

So, there is no need for you to be afraid or troubled. Nothing is impossible for God! Whatever you put your hand to will prosper. The pit and the prison are behind you. When God says He will lead you somewhere, you can trust Him to do it because He has it all under control.

Your life is now the grain pile.

AFTERWORD

RECEIVE THE BLESSING

Jesus came to give you the blessing. The Bible says that whoever calls upon the name of Jesus has the legal right to become a citizen of His great Kingdom and a member of His household.

Your life will truly begin to prosper when you make the decision to enter the covenant of Abraham through Jesus Christ.

As a son or daughter of the house, you have a great inheritance. Since Jesus paid the price for you, you can receive the whole thing simply by asking.

Then, your life becomes a matter of learning about your rights and how the Kingdom operates—and you begin to apply those laws and walk it out.

Today can be the day that you change direction and receive the blessing and promise of God. This can be the day that you say "Yes" to Jesus. All you need to do is simply acknowledge you want and need God in your life.

Pray this out loud:

> *"Father, You said in the Bible that if I call on the name of Jesus, You will receive me, make me brand-new on the inside, fill me with your Holy Spirit, and teach me how to live in Your Kingdom.*
>
> *I need that! So let it be recorded in heaven that I now call on the name of Jesus and ask Jesus to be my Lord and Savior. Today, I receive Your salvation and all the goodness included with it. And I thank you for that, in the mighty name of Jesus. Amen."*

ABOUT THE AUTHOR

Gary Keesee is a television host, author, international speaker, financial expert, successful entrepreneur, and pastor who has made it his mission to help people win in life, especially in the areas of faith, family, and finances.

After years of living in poverty, Gary and his wife, Drenda, discovered the principles of the Kingdom of God, and their lives were drastically changed. Together, under the direction of the Holy Spirit, they created several successful businesses and paid off all of their debt. Now, they spend their time declaring the Good News of the Kingdom of God around the world through Faith Life Now, their organization that exists to motivate, educate, and inspire people from all walks of life and backgrounds to pursue success, walk out their God-designed purposes, and leave positive spiritual and moral legacies for their families.

Faith Life Now produces two television programs—*Fixing the Money Thing* and *Drenda*—as well as practical resources, conferences, and speaking events around the world.

Gary is also the president and founder of Forward Financial Group and the founding pastor of Faith Life Church, which has campuses in New Albany and Powell, Ohio.

Gary and Drenda, their five adult children and their spouses, and their grandchildren all reside in Central Ohio.

For additional resources by both Gary and Drenda, visit FaithLifeNow.com.

FINANCIAL REVOLUTION CONFERENCES

If you're a pastor or leader in your church, you probably have plenty of vision for your ministry. But do you have the money or resources you need to support the vision?

If your church is like most churches, the answer is probably *not quite* or even *no.*

Why?

We've found one of the biggest reasons is DEBT. So many Christians are being held *hostage* by debt.

Your people *WANT* to financially support the ministry and vision of your church, but many of them are living paycheck to paycheck with no hope of breaking free.

We can help.

For more than 25 years now, we've been working with churches of all sizes, helping them reach their goals and see their visions for their ministries become reality. And the best part is that this is completely free!

We help churches by helping their people. We can help *your church* by helping *your people*.

Learn more at **ftmtevent.com**.

Gary Keesee went from being completely desperate financially and physically to healthy and whole, paying cash for cars, building his home free from debt, starting multiple companies, and teaching hundreds of thousands of people about Kingdom living each week through television, ministry, and books just like this one.

What changed for Gary and how can it change YOUR LIFE?

Your answers are in the pages of THIS book series.

This isn't just another set of books with tips on how to fix your finances.

Full of fresh revelation, powerful examples from the Word of God, and inspiring personal stories about Gary and others who applied the foundational teachings from these five Kingdom principles in their own lives and experienced drastic change as a result, this series of books was written to help YOU experience real change in EVERY area of your life.

No matter your situation, there are answers. It's never too late.

You can have your own amazing story!

Join Gary Keesee on this incredible five-part journey of discovery that will completely revolutionize YOUR life... just like it did his.

This set contains paperback versions of Gary's complete *Your Financial Revolution* book series:

- *Your Financial Revolution: The Power of Allegiance*
- *Your Financial Revolution: The Power of Rest*
- *Your Financial Revolution: The Power of Strategy*
- *Your Financial Revolution: The Power of Provision*
- *Your Financial Revolution: The Power of Generosity*

Get your copy of the complete *Your Financial Revolution* five-book series at GaryKeesee.com.

Made in the USA
Monee, IL
26 November 2023